The Satin Entanglement

Shivani Shrivastva

BookLeaf Publishing

India | USA | UK

Presentation by *BookLeaf Publishing*

Web: www.bookleafpub.com

E-mail: info@bookleafpub.com

ISBN: 9789360941925

First edition 2024

*To my Dear Readers and all the poetry
enthusiasts out there,*

*This book is dedicated to you, who have always
appreciated the power of words and the beauty
they hold.*

*You have been my constant source of
encouragement, cheering me on through every
step of my journey. Your love for poetry has
kept the art alive, and I am grateful to be a part
of this amazing community.*

*To my Mom and Dad, I dedicate my first book
of poetry. Your unwavering support and trust
have always encouraged me to do better and
fearlessly follow my spontaneous mind and
heart.*

*To the Universe and Life itself, I dedicate this
book, for they have been my greatest
inspirations. The mysteries and wonders of life
have always captivated me, and I have tried to
capture its essence through my words.*

*To those who are often unheard, unseen, or
unappreciated, I dedicate my book to you.*

Through this collection of poetry, I hope to touch your hearts and souls and inspire you to look beyond the surface, to see the beauty in the mundane, and to cherish every moment of life.

May you find solace, comfort, and inspiration in the words woven with care, empathy, and love.

Thank you for being a part of this beautiful journey of self-discovery and expression.

With love and gratitude,

Shivani Shrivastva

ACKNOWLEDGEMENT

Dear Readers,

I am filled with gratitude as I hold my poetry book in my hands, and it is only because of you that this dream of mine has come true. Your constant support, encouragement, and appreciation have been the driving force behind this accomplishment. Thank you for taking the time to read my words and giving them a chance to touch your hearts.

To Bookleaf Publishing, thank you for believing in me and giving me the opportunity to share my art with the world. Your unwavering support and guidance have helped me turn my dream into a reality, and I am forever grateful.

To my Dad, thank you for being my rock and always encouraging me to pursue my dreams. Your unwavering support, love, and guidance have been my anchor through all the ups and downs of this journey.

Lastly, to my intuition, thank you for always guiding me towards my true calling. You have been my constant companion, and without your nudges, I might never have discovered my passion for poetry.

Thank you, everyone, for being a part of my journey as a poetess. I hope my words continue to touch your hearts and inspire you to chase your own dreams.

With love and gratitude,
Your Poetess, Shivani (Shi)

PREFACE

The room was dimly lit, and a young girl of thirteen sat at her study table, struggling to solve a mathematical equation. Her study table was right in the center of the dining hall, a place she dreaded. She could be easily monitored from anywhere in the small two-bedroom house, which she found suffocating. Despite being a wild soul, her free spirit was not always appreciated by those around her. Perhaps they feared the power she possessed, the capability of stirring the tides of the ocean with her tiny bare fingers.

As she sat staring at the darkness in front of her, a sudden light of poetry shone upon her. Flipping through the pages of her notebook, she began to write. Something had ignited within, a spark of creativity that reminded her of her potential to create something great. Her pen took flight, and the pages transformed into feathers, her mind becoming light and her soul set ablaze.

Within minutes, she had written her very first poem, and she could hardly believe her eyes. Her hands trembled with excitement, and she glanced around to see if anyone had noticed the widest smile on her face. In that moment, when she longed for someone to share her joy with, she found herself alone. Yet, her heart fluttered with pride, and she felt a sense of accomplishment that she had never felt before.

From that day on, she found refuge in her pen and paper. She used words to express her experiences, observations, and emotions. Her heart laughed, danced, skipped, and fell, and she captured all these moments in her writing.

Every unobserved thing, every unnoticed person, became her muse, and her art and words blossomed into a beautiful journey of poetry.

As I sit here twelve years later and look back on those teenage years, I am grateful for the gift of writing. It has become a part of who I am, and I am honored to share my first poetry book with you all.

I hope that as you read these poems, you can feel the passion and love that went into creating them. I hope that they touch your heart in the way that they have touched mine. And most of all, I hope that they inspire you to see the beauty in the world around you and to appreciate the little things that often go unnoticed.

Thank you for joining me on this journey, and I am excited to see where it takes us next.

An Ode to My Parents' Love

Through fights and tantrums, to laying in each
other's arms,
Through cries and annoyance, to goofily smiling
at each other,
From pulling each other's legs, to soulfully
listening to one another,
My parents, individually and together showed,
How slow love can power through.

Love has its way of showing itself in the little
details of comprehension and safety,
It shows itself in warmth and integrity.
It shows itself in the passage of time and the
aching wait for someone.
Moreover, it shows itself in slow consistency
and sweet surrender.

I've seen my parents drive through whatever it
took to make their marriage
work gracefully for decades.
I've seen them quietly hurting when they
couldn't bring themselves up to
talk to one another, yet always reaching out for
each other.

I've seen what laughter and cries look like,
together.
I've seen what intimacy and self-worth looks
like, together.
I've seen what respect feels like,
I've seen what chaos looks like.
I've seen it all, through them.
And for all I can say...

Love is like the Moon.
It has its phases.

Sometimes you can never see it, but you know
it's there.
Sometimes it is an eclipse, so beautiful yet brutal
when seen with naked eye,
Sometimes it is bright in the night sky where it
guides the unknown and
Sometimes it's just...there, looking at you too.

My Dad has shown me in every way, what and
how men are supposed to be like.
He has shown me what I deserve and how
worthy am I.
My Mom has shown me how to fiercely and
fearlessly face the world,
She has shown me what strength looks like in a
woman.

My parents are not perfect, but beautiful when
they are together,
They are not perfect, but so effortlessly,
complement each other.
If this is what love looks like, even after years
and decades,
With certainty, I can say...
"Getting one's heart broken in love till you find
your imperfect one, is all worth it."

Threaded

I love how our human experiences are not what
we perceive them to be.

I love when I am able to think that my
personality is my own, but truly it's not.
My entire life, I have been trying to find the
perfect me, until now.

I know my existence is my favorite garment, and
is threaded by strings from everyone that I have
ever met.
I find myself to be a beautiful amalgamation of
every soul whom I have crossed paths with.

I seldom catch myself, laughing like the little
girl whom I saw laughing last week,

Or find myself smirking the exact same way like
the cute coffeehouse guy I met a month ago.
Or can sense my dialect match with my favorite
character in a TV show.

We tend to live in their world for a short period
of time,
Experiencing little specs of their existence in our
own mind.
It is such a beautiful feeling to be all and
everyone at some point of our lives.

It is incredible if you think how,
In this world with billions of souls walking the
earth,
We are blessed to hold hands of a few hundreds.
We get this wonderful opportunity to know
certain people to their vast depths,
Who then, on our favorite garment of existence,
leave their imprints.

No matter, we think we are replaceable, and
something which is very true,
But there's one tiny little thing that we miss
acknowledging,
'Our threads have intertwined with theirs too.'

And no matter how hard we try to forget each
other; we won't be.

It is a bittersweet feeling.
If you look at it with a different perspective I guess,
It is something which makes us realize how valuable we are,
How valuable connections and this life itself is.

Not the Usual Welcome

What is that something, that moves you and
makes you
notice things that have duly gone unnoticed?
Something that is just heard or seen but never
felt?

For me it would be when I hear a "Thank you"
back, from a person
whom I thanked.

It is a small thing.
Nothing special.
But it also doesn't come from common masses.

It comes from a person or small set of people
who appreciate
you for giving them a small chance to help or
serve you.

A small chance to show that they are worthy and
capable.
A small chance to support their livelihood.
It comes from people who feel acknowledged
and are humble.
It comes from people who work hard in the sun
stacking
bricks to construct a building.
It comes from the person who removes dead
leaves from the
road and someone who refills the tank.

To hear a "Thank you" back, instead of a
Welcome, is so
unusual.
It made me stop and think.

It never occurred to me that a thing so small
would make me
want to write something.
Something that I could have easily nodded to as
a reply and gone
about doing my work.

Something I could have, maybe, just heard and
never felt.
It is unusual but beautiful.
I will remember that person.

This Is What Scares You

Once, an old man sitting next to a young woman
asked,
"What is the thing that scares
you the most, young lady?"

His voice low and gruff, jolted the sweet woman
from a long trance like state.
She had been sitting there lost, with eyes dark
and blank staring into an empty space.
She turned to her side to find herself
accompanied by a very old
but a wise looking man.

She looked into his droopy old eyes,
Tracing the lines on her palm and solemnly
replied

"I do not fear anything, sir."

The old man smiled and said,
"Your eyes… your eyes say something else,
young lady.
Your eyes are glistening with battles which your
heart has
nurtured for months.

Your quivering lips shows that you have craved
truth
from lying minds, which has broken you a
thousand times.
Your soul, so strong, which protects you from
the wrath of
silly minds have shut down your tone for
closure, as you
have become a warrior.

Your palms, the lines on them which you keep
tracing are nothing but counting's
of how many left you stranded on the unspoken
road.
Your mind, my young lady is the tangled
universe of
your reflection that you so dearly love.

You are nothing but a supernova, ready to burst
into rebirth of million young selves,

Dear lady, you are the light, so bright, not many can
seize in their small hands,
You are the warmth not many can bask in,
You are the language of love, not many can understand,
and that is what,
Scares you the most."

Men in Love

Men in Love are my favorite.

I admire when I see a man in love.
He is so different.
So very different from the crowd, you could
easily spot him.
He is different in ways his heart commands his
actions.
He is different in ways his eyes would glide over
you in pure admiration.
The kind of man who wouldn't just give up on
you.
The kind of man, who isn't perfect but knows
acceptance.
Such is a man in love.

The kind of man who wears his heart on his
sleeves and yet can
command respect from those around.
The kind of man who would be cold, yet rub
your feet to keep you warm.

The kind of man who is respectful in his touch
and gentle with his words.
The kind of man who is careful and does not
care any less.
The kind of man who would stand up for you in
your absence,
And hold you close and dance in front of his
companions.
Such is a man in love.

A man who is not afraid to express, a man who
is not afraid to show.
A man who is so full and complete that he only
wants to treat you.
A man who would fix your crown and kiss you.
The kind of man who would let you walk in
front, while secretly
protecting and having your back.

I love Men in Love.
These are the kind of men the world needs more
of.
The respectful and sincere ones.

One who knows to stand his ground and yet be
modest.
The one who is capable of understanding and is
open.
The one who knows the value of his woman.
The one who has patience and resilience.
The one who is calm and peaceful.
He is the kind of man who is competent.

It does not take a superman to fall in love, but
takes a real man to be in love.

Men in love are the ones whose happiness lies in
keeping you safe and secure,
The ones whose happiness lies in kissing away
your tears.
They are the ones who would always let you
play your favorite song whenever you hit the
road.
And would always be patient with you and look
beyond your fears.

The one who admires you, for your mind,
The one who is compassionate and kind.
The one who could literally move mountains,
just to see you smile.
The one who knows his own worth,
The one who could remind you of yours when
you stumble and fall.

These are the men who are secretly changing the
world.

The ones in whose presence you can feel so at
peace.
Men in love are the ones who make sure of your
well-being.
The one who doesn't harbor hate and resentment,
The one who would be broken, yet can get back
up with passion and
tenderness.
The kind of man who is masculine enough to
love again.

These are the men, I adore.
Men in Love, oh! You have my heart,
I love 'Men in love,' who give their all.

Metamorphosis

There is something sweet about being destroyed.

To be carried around aimlessly by a gust of
wind,
To fall and to shatter,
To burn slowly like an ember on fire.
To flow down the cascade of dear misery,
And choke on the daunting melancholy.

There's something beautiful about getting our
hearts broken. Again.
To go through the dreaded loop of immense
sorrow and pain.
The ache that makes us feel sick to the stomach,
The howl of the soul deafening our ears.

Oh, the Familiarity!

These are the moments of extreme low,
Our tired eyes search for meaning in places once
considered shallow.
The mind tries to make sense of the fleeting
time,
The scare if we will ever resurface and see the
light.

Such is moment when only the subconscious
comprehends,
A cycle of renewal, gratification and slow
metamorphosis.

When the wings are lost to clippers or fights,
There is something very wild about just lying in
the battlefield looking
at the sky.
The feeling of liberation that creeps in,
The feeling which beckons to us lending a hand
of resurrection.

Oh, the Freedom!

We know it in our bones that we will survive.
There's something very bold about not fearing to
be destroyed.

For we have transformed.
For we have survived.

And when the time comes, to face our demons,
We won't run or hide.
We will again burn to ashes,
And gallantly, we will rise.

Swish Swish Swish

It's 6 in the morning.
I am in my bed, cozied up inside my blanket.
It's chilly, outside.
The sun's rays barely make it to the dewy leaves,
which glisten as the wind
blows past them.

I am half asleep and I can hear morning bhajans
put on by my father as he goes
about getting ready for his office.
I hear a faint brush of the broom from behind
me, outside the window.
It's my neighbor.

He wakes up at this hour everyday and
religiously brushes away the fallen leaves from
his backyard.
The rhythmic stroke of the broom, as if painting
on the wet soil, falls in sync

with my half sleepy fingers gently repeating his
motions on my bed sheet.
'Swish, swish, swish'

He spends three hours daily, going about
grooming his garden and terrace.
He will collect the fallen leaves, clean the area
around the well, tidy up the terrace,
water the few rose plants, fill up the water tanks,
and clean up the small drain.
He would do this each day.

His house, which used to be my frequent when I
was a little girl is now just a
place, I see him do his work, silently.
He has a wife who works at a pharmacy and a
daughter who used to be my playmate, now a
graduate, lives in another city.
Everyday, his wife would go to work and he
would tidy up.

The house is not very well-built and neither is
he.
Cement chipping off the roof, iron rods sticking
out, canopy hanging loosely,
grills and rods rusted.
I remember how it looks from the inside.
Nothing much has changed.

Of the little that I can see from my window, the
house remains the same.
Silent.

I don't quite know where he goes or does after
those three hours. I barely see
anyone.

I rarely see his wife on the terrace, laying out
clothes to dry, on the parapet wall.
She would secure the clothes with small stones
to prevent them from flying away by
the breeze.
She is a sweet lady.
She would call out to me whenever she would
see me in my lawn.
We would exchange conversations about our
whereabouts, to which her answers
would always be consistent.
"I am doing well" and "Life, it's the same."
We would then exchange a smile and she would
go inside, and I would be left thinking about the
last line,
"It's the same."

It's the same.
Night falls and a bulb lights up the front porch
of the house.
It's dim.

There's no motion to be seen.
But as soon as the morning rays hit its broken
walls, I hear my neighbor again.
It is almost as if he sets up the space for a visitor
not seen by anyone.

He would go about cleaning the backyard,
collecting leaves, tidying up, and my
fingers would still follow his rhythm…
Swish…Swish...Swish...

One Time

Isn't it crazy how one particular time can be so
different for humanity as whole.

Sitting on a sky-high patio, I think to myself,
What must others be doing at this very moment?

Some might be having a hot sip of chocolate
coffee after a long day at work,
While some must be playing with their little
ones,
Some might be struggling to open a jar,
While some might be dreaming of a place wild
and far.

Some might be making sweet love for the first
time,
While some might be crying within but be
hiding behind a tender smile,
While some might be confessing their love,
While some might be shying away from the
thought of their crush.

It is so strange while I eye the endless night sky
above me and feel the soft tender
breeze grazing through my skin,
I smile and think,
"What it would be like to walk down the nightly
road, holding hands with someone
while a stranger would eye us from his window,
and recall days when he did the same?"

The Girl in the Auto Rickshaw

Her skin was brushing against mine as the auto
rickshaw revved and bumped
against the speed breakers.
Her arm felt smooth and firm as the vehicle
rhythmically jolted through the traffic.

She didn't care to move her arm neither did I.
Maybe, she thought she felt safe in a woman's
presence.
Or maybe she didn't care at all.
I looked at her.
I could only see a part of her face lit up
beautifully by the morning sun as she leaned
against the rickshaw's compartment wall.

Her hair was flowy, waving as the wind flew
past it.
It was smooth.
I could see her earrings dangling and swirling
with the wind.

I looked back at her arm.
I looked at hers and I looked at mine.
We both were so similar.
The texture, the teeny tiny waxed hair, the mole,
everything…same.
The skin color, that was different.

I looked at her clothes and then mine.
We both were dressed in the money we could
afford.
Our footwears were not the same either.
I was in heels and she was in a simple strap
sandal.
But the toe nails, they were the same.
The skin on it was the same.
She was wearing nail paint which had chipped
away a bit. My nails were
done fresh and groomed.
She wore a watch. The kind of watches I used to
wear years ago, but
now only dandy ones.
But our palms were the same.
The lines on them, similar.

She just sat there, facing away from me and
looking outside.
She was thinking, thinking about something.
Did she think that someone would be noticing
her?
Did she think of herself to be noticeable?

She was focused on something.
Something I couldn't see.
And I was focused on her.

She felt so different yet so similar.
Her arm was still touching mine.
It was warm, smooth and beautiful.
I was happy that I could feel it.
She got off at a place I don't quite remember.
And then, she turned back and I saw her.

She was so much like me.

She didn't quiet care to look anywhere else
rather than giving changes to the
rickshaw driver.
I kept looking at her and watched as she drifted
off into the crowd.

I will remember her.
But won't be remembered.

Such a funny feeling, isn't it?

She was noticed.

She was a beautiful young woman.
Though we both lived different lives, under
different segments of the society, we
were so much alike under our appearances.

I still wonder what she was thinking.
Maybe this is what she has gifted me,
"A thing to think about her and
remember her as 'The Girl in the Auto
Rickshaw.'"

Will You?

Will you hold my hand when I would not be able
to hold myself?
Will you try to understand the mess I am made
of?
Will you look into my eyes and say that I am
safe with you?
Will you have my back when I lose my sight?
Will you love me through my flaws and make
me fall in love again?
Will you show me the world with your unbiased
perception?
Will you run and hug me tight when you see me
sitting in a lone corner?
Will you at last, kiss me and let me know that
you are going to be there forever?
Will you…?

We Are All the Same

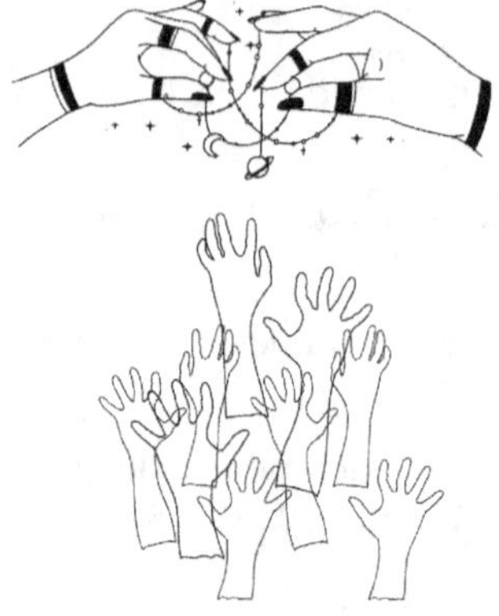

Existence is a work of art.
A journey into the unknown.
The sand of time tickling down the glass.
The measure of what's good and what's not.

One carries himself like an artist painting hues
of misery into the blank canvas
of his life.
Creating sculptures of war and peace and
displaying them in museums
of his mind.
With every stroke of his brush, he paints himself
in the color of nature, being
completely oblivious to what it has to offer.
A tiny life merely existing through space and
time fulfilling his destiny before he

dies.

A man is an amazing object of the universe.
A perfect model with the ability to think in any
dimension.
He creates stories of life and death, printing
them in books to be remembered and
read.
He who sits by the river, and wonders, what can
he leave behind and what can he take.
He who watches everyone and creates fables of
their life.
For him existence is just a show of time.
He who walks down the memory lane followed
by his shadows.
He strives at every point to run and has an
undying desire
to be better than the others.

He who can compete and contemplate, he who
can taste the sourness of his actions.
A man is so fond of rewards, that he created
evil, only to later curse the destruction.
The beauty and ugliness of self which he truly
tries to understand, leaves him
hungry for more.
He who decorates himself with silver and gold is
just as hollow to his core.

Man is nothing, but a vessel.
He has the power to love and to curse, to admire
and to loathe.
In search of his own meaning and purpose, he
questions his worth.
He writes and paints, he sings and dances.
He who fights and destroys,
He is a human and so am I.

She and Herself

It was for her essence that she fell in love so
deeply.

The way she masked her shadows and validated
her own beauty.
She comforted her secrets and let herself rest in
peace.
She was twined in a web of lustrous love so
heavenly, that
even the angels prayed for their wellbeing.

She kept her hidden from the world, and painted
herself with
the colors of joy and care.
She drew her form on every corner of the street,
For when the darkness would surface, they
would walk her home to safety.

She had become a persuader, cajoling herself to
rise above the rest,
She had become a writer, threading words of
strength and courage onto her fate.
She would pluck stars and blow it into her eyes,
so that
she could see the world, high above from the
sky.

She shone so bright, enough to light up the
northern firmament swallowed in complete
darkness.
She had become a musician who would sing to
the
melody and dance in the quirkiness of her
presence.

She was so in love with herself that even the
people envied 'The Duet.'

The Irony of Life

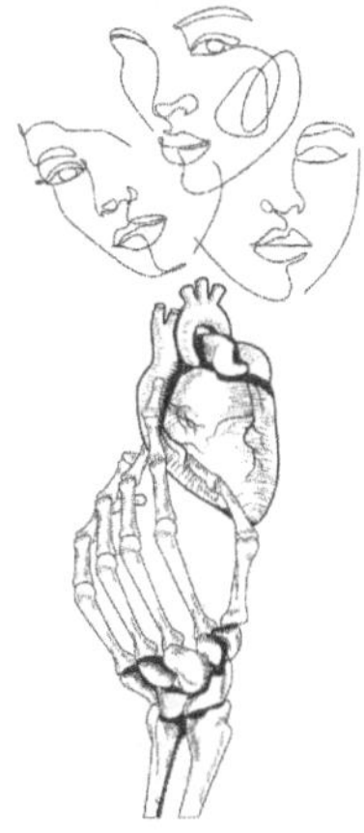

Isn't it ironic that the best masterpieces, like a beautiful song or
heart touching poetries are created when one is broken?

Isn't it ironic that people who are at the giving end is so clumsily acknowledged,
and certain times have to go through untamed hatred and complications,
only to end up having no idea of what lies ahead of them?

Isn't it ironic that individuals who are damaged like a cracked glass

tend to know the depth of the ground on which
they are about to shatter anytime,
still move on with hope?

Isn't it astounding to know that such people exist
and yet live a life so silent and are duly unheard
of?

Mankind is delusional.

We get carried away so easily by superficial
waves of biased
thinking and tend to overlook the pearls of
reality and truth
which lies buried at a finger's movement.

Unfortunately,
In this huge sardonic stage, with changing
phases and faces,
Souls can only switch between characters and
motives in a life so inevitable,
Only to find themselves on the deathbed of
grudges and succumb to the regret of their
decisions.

The Fisherman

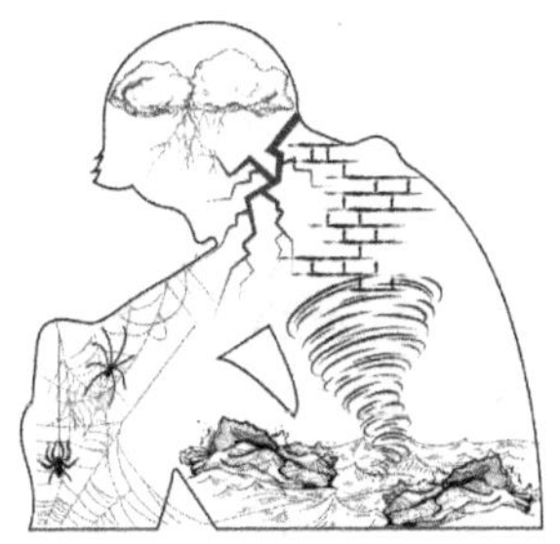

There are a few days when I come across certain
people who leave an
everlasting impression on my mind.
Without any conversation or interaction, they
seldom strike a chord in
my heart and I am left thinking about them.

They are the ones whom I would most likely
never cross paths with, again.
The ones who fleet away as soon as I blink and I
have just seconds to capture them with my eyes.
Such people are the ones who make me realize
how fortunate I am to be able to put new
perspectives to life.

Such is a story of a fisherman whom I came
across yesterday while on
a casual drive-around the neighborhood.

While passing through a very busy local market,
bustling with people, vendors and vehicles,
My eyes wandered and jumped from face to face
until amongst all the noise, it rested on one
fisherman.

He was sitting right in the middle of all the
chaos and was surprisingly very silent.
He wasn't talking to anyone.
He wasn't moving at all.
His eyes were locked in a silent gaze.

I looked at his daily supplies.
He still had few fishes left to sell.
He didn't try to make any sale unlike other
fishermen who were busy scaling and slicing up
cold dead fishes and talking nonchalantly with
their customers.
He wasn't even trying to break his gaze from the
vast nothingness that
he had plunged into, unlike other people who
were so loud.

I wondered where he was lost.
I wondered what he was thinking.
He had a very solemn look on his face, his eyes
were dark and blank,
lips parted, jaws slightly clenched, fingers held
in a grasp, hands

resting loosely on his knees and he sat there
resting against the wall behind him.

I felt something.
Something that I could not put into words.
From amongst the wild noisy crowd, he caught
my attention by simply
doing nothing at all.

Even with no movements, he looked like a
vicious storm.
Even with his eyes blank, it looked deep like the
ocean.
Even with his hands resting loosely on his knees,
looked strong like
firm branches which could uproot anything.

I passed by him and like I said, within seconds
he vanished out of my sight,
He had left an impression on my mind.

As the vehicle crossed the market and into the
silent night,
The fisherman was still loud in my head.
I kept thinking about the look he had.

He seemed sad, lost, emotionless, numb and
everything all at once.

His mind was violent and it was louder than the
noisy crowd.
His cold visions were swirling in a vicious cycle
something that I could relate to by
looking how deep he had submerged in them.
His skin must've been cold just like those frozen
fishes.
Melancholy clung to him like a spider does to its
prey.

He must be contemplating.
What if his mother back home was dying or he
needed rent
to secure the house he was living in?
Or his children's school fees were pending or his
crops this month did not yield well?

As a person with considerable class difference, I
can only think of such problems in his life,
Something which I readily do not have to worry
about.
Maybe because I am not capable of it.

What if he was thinking about how to face his
wife and tell her that he might need the
entire saving to get some medicine for his dying
mother or how they would not be able
to buy groceries for the next day, or simply how
meaningless everything is.

I would never know what he was going through.
I would never know the answers to my
questions.
But I know this,
Whatever he was facing, can never be
comprehended by people with the likes of you
and me, who have very little to worry about.
To worry about things that might be insignificant
in our lives,
But for him, it meant like standing on the edge
and watching his life slowly chip away with the
passage of time.

The One Who Suffers

How strange the world goes by,
With every spoken word of disgrace,
The soul sublimes deep within the oceanic tide.

The waves of enmity tears apart the pearl of
love.
Only to find peace in the loneliest corners of the
earth.

Why is it that one has to stay silent and endure
deep scars
of humiliation,
Just to dissolve the hurricane of hate and protect
themselves from further destruction?

How long can a person hold back from crashing
into the
realm of disgust,
Fabricating their true emotions with a solemn
smile and a
heavy heart?

Fragile Ego

Oh, to tame it,
To protect it,
A task it is.

Oh, to sculpt it,
With every experience,
A task it is.

To carry it like glass, and a heart full of pride,
A task it is.
For when it smashes,
It hurts bad
And makes you want to burn bridges.

To see and feel yourself turn into a vengeful
monster,
To breathe fire and chew on its shards and wish
blood on others.
Hoping for a comeback so spiteful and savage,
Your eyes burn with rage and you clench your
jaws and fist into a
deadly embrace.

To collect it back, it's a shame
But you still insist on mending it

with glass is foolish.

For you can never tame it, or protect it.
It will swallow you whole.
You won't be a human anymore
if you do not learn,
But a carrier of fragile ego,
Till you see yourself burn.

Days like This

I like days when I wake up with no thoughts in
my mind.

The silent mornings, the crisp winter air, light
fog that lingers around the garden and the tiny
rays of sunshine penetrating through the clouds.
I like days when my morning tea doesn't get cold
too quickly and my blanket is still warm.
I like days when I stay away from the chaos in
my mind and let
myself float in the sweet melody of earthly
sounds.

I like days when a stranger smiles at me and I
feel seen,
When little kids go to school across the street,
laughing and jumping.

When old ladies and men carry broken branches
to give its death a new meaning,
I like days when I greet and talk to the flowers in
my garden and they respond by swaying and
nodding.

When fallen leaves swirl up in the air by a gust
of wind, dancing to its rhythm.
I like days when the soil smells fresh and little
insects and
animals wholeheartedly rejoice in them.

I like days when I get the opportunity to feel the
energy of
nature on my face, which warms and cools me at
the same time.
I like days when my entire family is home,
going about their work, talking and singing, with
faces shining bright from a sweet smile.

Everything feels so alive.

I like days when the peace within me pours out
and I can feel
it's tangible miracle and bliss, manifesting in the
world around me in real time.

My Old Lover

Tell me oh, my old lover,
Why is that when I see pretty poppies bloom, I
think
of you?

Tell me oh, my old lover,
Why is that when my coffee
turns cold, I still look to your side and imagine
your face with lips wide in a smile, hands held
out and hear you say,
"Give me, I'll warm it up
for you."?

Why is that when a star shoots in the night sky,
I dream of us in a wonderland with just fairies
and
fireflies?

Why is that when I turn to your side of bed, I
can still feel
your prints running rhythmically through the
sheets?
Oh, tell me my old lover,
Why is that when I look in the rearview mirror, I
see us both running in the field of dandelions but
only this time we run
away from the present?

Tell me, my old lover, why is that when I hear
someone sing, I close my eyes and see your lips
move in sync with the lyrics?

Do you still want me close? Or is it just me?

Tell me, my old lover,
Do you still recall the good times
Or is it just me, swirling through time trying to
forget
you?

Is it just me, who would not give you a chance
but

still want to touch you?
Is it just me, who has moved on and won't look
back
but seldom re-read old chapters just to smile?

The Child Who Fought Alone

I wish someone could tell you what it feels like
to be
appreciated,
I wish someone could show you what innocent
love is,
I wish the little you was held close to heart,
I wish you never had these scars.

You were very young when you saw the world in
ways you
shouldn't have.

Your little palms had to carry the weight of
criticism,
You were very little when you were subjected to
words so harsh
that my mind yet cannot fathom.
You long for appreciation, you long for
validation, that, I
know.

I wish you get these in your adult years,
The acceptance and the feeling of belongingness
which you have craved for so long.

You solemnly and quietly had to endure all the
pain while your heart still aches
whenever the trigger is released.
I wish you could thread your feelings and shout
it into the galaxy,
Hoping for someone to hear and acknowledge
your existence.
For someone to show love and respect that you
deserve,
For someone to sit close by and truly listen to
your words.

I wish you get blessed in ways you are destined
to,
I wish, you do not have to cry softly amongst the
oblivious crowd,
I wish someone out there notices your eyes; I
wish someone out
there would wipe away the agonizing cries.

I wish I could show you what you mean to this
world,
There are people who look up to you to get a
gentle reminder of
Tender Love.

Love, you are hurting, that, I know.
I wish I could be the adult by your side and hold
you really, really close.

The Path

Into an unknown quest for epiphany,
I maneuvered through the sublime chaos of
self-reflection.

Letting the bands of resentment dwindle into the
nightly errand,
I chose a path, marked by an unsettling urge to
manifest novel
perception.

Remember the Rose

Let not the rose of love fall out of care when we
drift apart,
Let not the rose of passion succumb when you
see me
with someone else.
As we both know what our destiny has to offer,
Let not the rose in your hand slip into the deep
abyss of
regret.

Had only you been in my place would you have
known,
how difficult it is for me to move on,
Let not the rose pass away when I bid you my
final
goodbye,

Let not the petals droop, even when your love
subsides.

I handed you this rose as a promise to keep you
close to
my heart,
Not knowing that it is not plastic and will perish
after I am long gone,
Still, I pray you to keep its fragrance in your
mind alive,
For when it would bloom again, you'll know I'm
still there,
somewhere, close by.